"The right to religious freedom is not optional but essential."

—**POPE LEO XIV**, October 10, 2025

The new 2026–2027 *Handbook and Planning Guide* is designed to support and inspire you in your ministry throughout the year. As you explore the calendar pages, you will notice a special focus on religious liberty, a theme close to the heart of the Church and especially meaningful as we celebrate the 250th anniversary of the United States in 2026. This year's planner features selected passages from *Dignitatis Humanae*, the Second Vatican Council's declaration on religious freedom.

May these reflections enrich your planning, deepen your prayer, and strengthen your ministry in the year ahead.

David Dziena
Vice President of Publishing,
Bayard

Catechist

EDITORS: Erika de Urquidi, David Dziena
CREATIVE DIRECTOR: Ted Schluenderfritz
ADVERTISING AND SALES: Emmanuelle Beauvillain
PRODUCTION: Kevin Jensen

bayard

Pflaum Publishing Group

If you have any question or comment, or to inquire about placing an order, please contact:

Service@pflaum.com
1-800-558-2292 (8AM–6PM ET)
1564 Fencorp Dr., Fenton, MO 63026-2942

COVER IMAGES: (PIER GIORGIO FRASSATI) RENÁTA SEDMÁKOVÁ, (BASILICA) JACLYN LIPPLEMAN, (ST. CARLO ACUTIS) JULIÁN IGLESIAS (CROWD) VYTAUTAS MARKŪNAS/CATHOPIC

WHAT'S INSIDE

NEW FOR 2026-2027

Gospel Weeklies

Pflaum FAITH FORMATION PROGRAM

FOR FAMILIES

Revised. Reimagined. Rooted in the Gospel.

FOR TEACHERS

FOR STUDENTS

Call us at (800) 543-4383
or visit gospelweeklies.com

Pflaum Gospel Weeklies is published by *Pflaum Publishing Group*, a division of Bayard USA bayard

Common Catholic Prayers and Practices

OUR FATHER

Our Father, who art in heaven, hallowed be thy name. Thy kingdom come. Thy will be done on earth as it is in heaven. Give us this day our daily bread, and forgive us our trespasses, as we forgive those who trespass against us, and lead us not into temptation, but deliver us from evil. Amen.

HAIL MARY

Hail Mary, full of grace. The Lord is with thee. Blessed art thou among women, and blessed is the fruit of thy womb, Jesus. Holy Mary, Mother of God, pray for us sinners, now and at the hour of our death. Amen.

GLORY BE

Glory be to the Father, and to the Son, and to the Holy Spirit, as it was in the beginning, is now, and ever shall be, world without end. Amen.

THE APOSTLES' CREED

I believe in God, the Father almighty, Creator of heaven and earth. And in Jesus Christ, his only Son, our Lord, who was conceived by the Holy Spirit, born of the Virgin Mary, suffered under Pontius Pilate, was crucified, died, and was buried. He descended into hell; the third day he arose again from the dead; he ascended into heaven, and sits at the right hand of God, the Father almighty, from thence he shall come to judge the living and the dead. I believe in the Holy Spirit, the holy Catholic Church, the communion of saints, the forgiveness of sins, the resurrection of the body, and life everlasting. Amen.

HAIL, HOLY QUEEN

Hail, Holy Queen, Mother of Mercy, our life, our sweetness and our hope. To thee do we cry, poor banished children of Eve. To thee do we send up our sighs, mourning and weeping in this valley of tears. Turn then, most gracious advocate, thine eyes of mercy toward us, and after this our exile, show unto us the blessed fruit of thy womb, Jesus. O clement, O loving, O sweet Virgin Mary. Amen.

PRAYER TO SAINT MICHAEL, THE ARCHANGEL

St. Michael the Archangel, defend us in battle, be our protection against the wickedness and snares of the Devil. May God rebuke him, we humbly pray. And do thou, O Prince of the Heavenly Host, by the Power of God, thrust into hell Satan and all evil spirits who wander the earth seeking the ruin of souls. Amen.

ANIMA CHRISTI

Soul of Christ, be my
sanctification.
Body of Christ, be my salvation.
Blood of Christ, fill all my veins.
Water of Christ's side, wash out
my stains.
Passion of Christ, my comfort be.
O good *Jesu*, listen to me.
In thy wounds I fain to hide,
N'er to be parted from thy side,
Guard me, should the foe
assail me.
Call me when my life shall
fail me.
Bid me come to thee above,
With thy saints to sing thy love,
World without end. Amen.

MEMORARE

Remember, O most gracious Virgin Mary, that never was it known that anyone who fled to thy protection, implored thy help, or sought thy intercession was left unaided. Inspired by this confidence, I fly unto thee, O Virgin of virgins my Mother. To thee do I come, before thee I stand, sinful and sorrowful. O Mother of the Word Incarnate, despise not my petitions, but in thy mercy hear and answer them. Amen.

THE ANGELUS

℣ The Angel of the Lord declared unto Mary.

℟ And she conceived by the Holy Spirit. (Hail Mary...)

℣ Behold the handmaid of the Lord.

℟ Be it done unto me according to thy word. (Hail Mary...)

℣ And the Word was made flesh.

℟ And dwelt among us. (Hail Mary...)

℣ Pray for us, O holy Mother of God.

℟ That we may be made worthy of the promises of Christ.

LET US PRAY: Pour forth, we beseech thee, O Lord, thy grace into our hearts; that we, to whom the Incarnation of Christ, thy Son, was made known by the message of an angel, may by his Passion and Cross be brought to the glory of his Resurrection. Through the same Christ, our Lord. Amen.

PHOTO: Eduardo Corcino/Adobe

ACT OF CONTRITION

O my God,
I am sorry and repent with all my heart
for all the wrong I have done
and for the good I have failed to do,
because by sinning I have offended you,
who are all good and worthy to be loved above all things.
I firmly resolve, with the help of your grace,
to do penance,
to sin no more,
and to avoid the occasions of sin.
Through the merits of the Passion of our Savior Jesus Christ,
Lord, have mercy.

(Order of Penance)

GRACE BEFORE MEALS

Bless us, O Lord, and these thy gifts, which we are about to receive from thy bounty, through Christ our Lord. Amen.

GRACE AFTER MEALS

We give thee thanks, for all thy benefits, Almighty God, who live and reign forever. Amen. May the souls of the faithful departed, through the mercy of God, rest in peace. Amen.

PRAYER TO ONE'S GUARDIAN ANGEL

Angel of God, my guardian dear, to whom God's love commits me here, ever this day (or night) be at my side, to light and guard, to rule and guide. Amen.

The Works of Mercy

THE CORPORAL WORKS OF MERCY

- Feed the hungry.
- Give drink to the thirsty.
- Clothe the naked.
- Visit the imprisoned.
- Shelter the homeless.
- Visit the sick.
- Bury the dead.
- Care for Creation*

THE SPIRITUAL WORKS OF MERCY

- Convert the sinner.
- Instruct the ignorant.
- Counsel the doubtful.
- Comfort the sorrowful.
- Bear wrongs patiently.
- Forgive all injuries.
- Pray for the living and the dead.
- Care for Creation*

*In an address on the 2016 World Day of Prayer for Creation, Pope Francis suggested "care for creation" as a new work of mercy, describing it as a "complement" to the existing works. Francis characterized this new work as having both corporal and spiritual components.

Mysteries of the Rosary

THE JOYFUL MYSTERIES

Traditionally prayed on Mondays, Saturdays, and, during the season of Advent, on Sundays:

- The Annunciation
- The Visitation
- The Nativity
- The Presentation in the Temple
- The Finding in the Temple

THE LUMINOUS MYSTERIES

Traditionally prayed on Thursdays:

- The Baptism of Christ in the Jordan
- The Wedding Feast at Cana
- Jesus' Proclamation of the Coming of the Kingdom of God
- The Transfiguration
- The Institution of the Eucharist

THE SORROWFUL MYSTERIES

Traditionally prayed on Tuesdays, Fridays, and, during the season of Lent, on Sundays:

- The Agony in the Garden
- The Scourging at the Pillar
- The Crowning with Thorns
- The Carrying of the Cross
- The Crucifixion and Death

THE GLORIOUS MYSTERIES

Traditionally prayed on Wednesdays and, outside the seasons of Advent and Lent, on Sundays:

- The Resurrection
- The Ascension
- The Descent of the Holy Spirit
- The Assumption of Mary
- The Coronation of Mary

The Ten Commandments

1. I am the Lord your God: you shall not have strange gods before me.
2. You shall not take the name of the Lord your God in vain.
3. Remember to keep holy the Lord's Day.
4. Honor your father and your mother.
5. You shall not kill.
6. You shall not commit adultery.
7. You shall not steal.
8. You shall not bear false witness against your neighbor.
9. You shall not covet your neighbor's wife.
10. You shall not covet your neighbor's goods.

The Seven Sacraments

SACRAMENTS OF INITIATION

In these sacraments, we meet Christ in profound ways and are initiated into the Christian life.

Baptism offers forgiveness of original sin and gives graces to begin a new life with Christ and the Church. It is the first sacrament.

Confirmation strengthens and deepens life in Christ and equips Christians with graces and gifts of the Holy Spirit to be witnesses for Christ.

Eucharist is supernatural nourishment in receiving the Body and Blood of Christ, to strengthen the Christian to follow Christ more closely.

SACRAMENTS AT THE SERVICE OF COMMUNION

Matrimony & Holy Orders are sometimes called sacraments of vocation. They call Christians to dedicate their lives both in communion with God and by loving service to others in specific ways.

SACRAMENTS OF HEALING

Penance/Reconciliation & Anointing of the Sick are sacraments through which Christians experience God's mercy and forgiveness of sins, as well as graces to help heal persons who may be suffering physically and/or spiritually.

Seven Themes of Catholic Social Teaching*

1. Life and dignity of the human person.
2. Call to family, community, and participation.
3. Rights and responsibilities.
4. Option for the poor and vulnerable.
5. The dignity of work and the rights of workers.
6. Solidarity.
7. Care for God's creation.

* Search "Themes of Catholic Social Teaching" at USCCB.org.

The Mass

The Sunday celebration of the Eucharist, traditionally known as the holy sacrifice of the Mass, is at the heart of the Church's life

Introductory Rites

- Entrance Antiphon
- Sign of the Cross and Greeting
- Rite of Blessing and Sprinkling of Holy Water
- Penitential Act
- *Gloria*
- Collect

Liturgy of the Word

- First Reading
- Responsorial Psalm
- Second Reading
- Gospel Acclamation
- Gospel
- Homily
- Profession of Faith
- Prayer of the Faithful

Liturgy of the Eucharist

- Preparation of the Gifts
- Prayer Over the Offerings
- Eucharistic Prayer
- Preface
- Holy, Holy, Holy (*Sanctus*)
- Memorial Acclamation
- Great Amen

Communion Rite

- Lord's Prayer
- Sign of Peace
- Fraction of the Bread (*Agnus Dei*)
- Communion
- Communion Antiphon
- Period of Silence or Song of Praise
- Prayer after Communion

Concluding Rite

- Blessing
- Dismissal

PHOTOS: (LEFT) AFRICA STUDIO/SHUTTERSTOCK (RIGHT) LightRocket via Getty Images

Celebrating the Liturgical Year

To celebrate the events in Christ's life, the mysteries of our faith, and our special love of our Blessed Mother, the Church has organized a three-year cycle of Scripture readings to be proclaimed at Sunday Mass. These cycles are referred to as Year A (focusing on the Gospel according to Matthew), Year B (focusing on the Gospel according to Mark and chapter 6 of the Gospel according to John), and Year C (focusing on the Gospel according to Luke). During the Easter season in all three years, we focus primarily on the Gospel according to John.

The Church year begins with the Season of Advent.

We are currently in Year A. Liturgical Year B (the 2026–2027 Liturgical Year) will begin on the First Sunday of Advent (November 29, 2026).

The Christmas Season follows Advent.

During this Liturgical Year, the Nativity of the Lord (12/25/2026) occurs on a Thursday. The Church will also celebrate the Holy Family of Jesus, Mary and Joseph (12/27/26), the Solemnity of Mary, the Holy Mother of God (1/1/2027), the Visit of the Magi (the Epiphany of the Lord (1/3/2027), and the Baptism of the Lord (1/10/27).

Then follows Ordinary Time and Lent.

Several weeks of Ordinary Time follow the Christmas season. Soon after, Lent begins on Ash Wednesday (2/10/27). The Triduum begins at sunset on Holy Thursday with the celebration of the Evening Mass of the Lord's Supper (3/25/2027) and concludes with vespers on Easter Sunday (3/28/2027).

The Easter Season follows Lent.

During the Easter season, the Gospels tell us of Jesus' post-Resurrection appearances; his teaching about his love as being that of a Good Shepherd; his naming of himself as the way, the truth, and the life; his promise not to leave us orphans; his prayer to the Father for us; and his Ascension. On Pentecost (5/16/2027), the Gospel tells us of the disciples receiving the Holy Spirit in the Upper Room.

The Season of Ordinary Time follows the Easter Season.

We will celebrate Ordinary Time for the remainder of the Liturgical Year. Through the weeks and months, the Gospels will proclaim Jesus' identity in different ways and tell of his miracles, parables, and teachings about the Kingdom of Heaven.

PHOTOS: (L-R, T-B) DEREK HATFIELD, PIXELDARKROOM, LARS HALLSTROM, LAURA_VN (ALL FROM SHUTTERSTOCK)

THE CHURCH YEAR has a special calendar. It doesn't go by months. It goes by seasons. Read about each season. Then color its section on the chart.

An Interactive Activity for Families

The Church Year begins with the season of Advent, which lasts about four weeks. It is a time of waiting and preparing for the birth of Jesus. **COLOR THE ADVENT SEASON VIOLET.**

The Christmas season lasts about three weeks. It is a time for joy. **COLOR THE CHRISTMAS SEASON WHITE OR GOLD.**

Between Christmas and Lent, there is a short period of Ordinary Time. During Ordinary Time, we hear about Jesus' life on earth. As we learn more about him, we grow closer to him. Green is the color of growth. **COLOR ORDINARY TIME GREEN.**

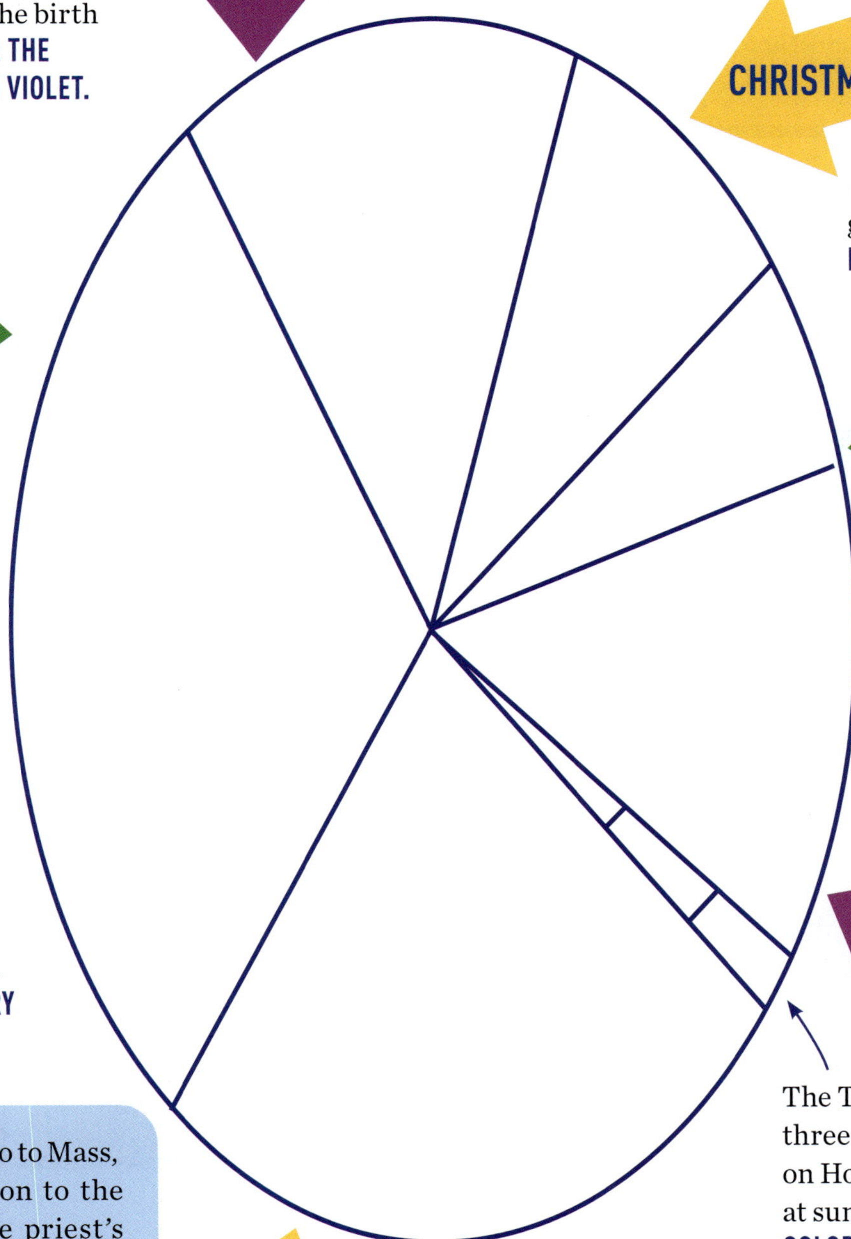

The rest of the year is a long period of Ordinary Time. It takes up most of the summer and fall. It is a time to grow closer to God every day. **COLOR ORDINARY TIME GREEN.**

Lent lasts six weeks. It is a season of penance and prayer as we near the time of Jesus' suffering and Death. **COLOR THE LENT SEASON VIOLET.**

The Triduum (meaning three days) begins at sunset on Holy Thursday and ends at sunset on Easter Sunday. **COLOR THE THREE SECTIONS OF THE TRIDUUM WHITE OR GOLD FOR HOLY THURSDAY, RED FOR GOOD FRIDAY, AND WHITE OR GOLD FOR HOLY SATURDAY/ EASTER SUNDAY.**

When you go to Mass, pay attention to the color of the priest's vestments. Except for certain special feasts or reasons, the priest's vestments will match the color of the season!

The Easter season is about seven weeks long. It ends on Pentecost. It is a joyful time. **COLOR THE EASTER SEASON WHITE OR GOLD.**

The Gospels TIMELINE

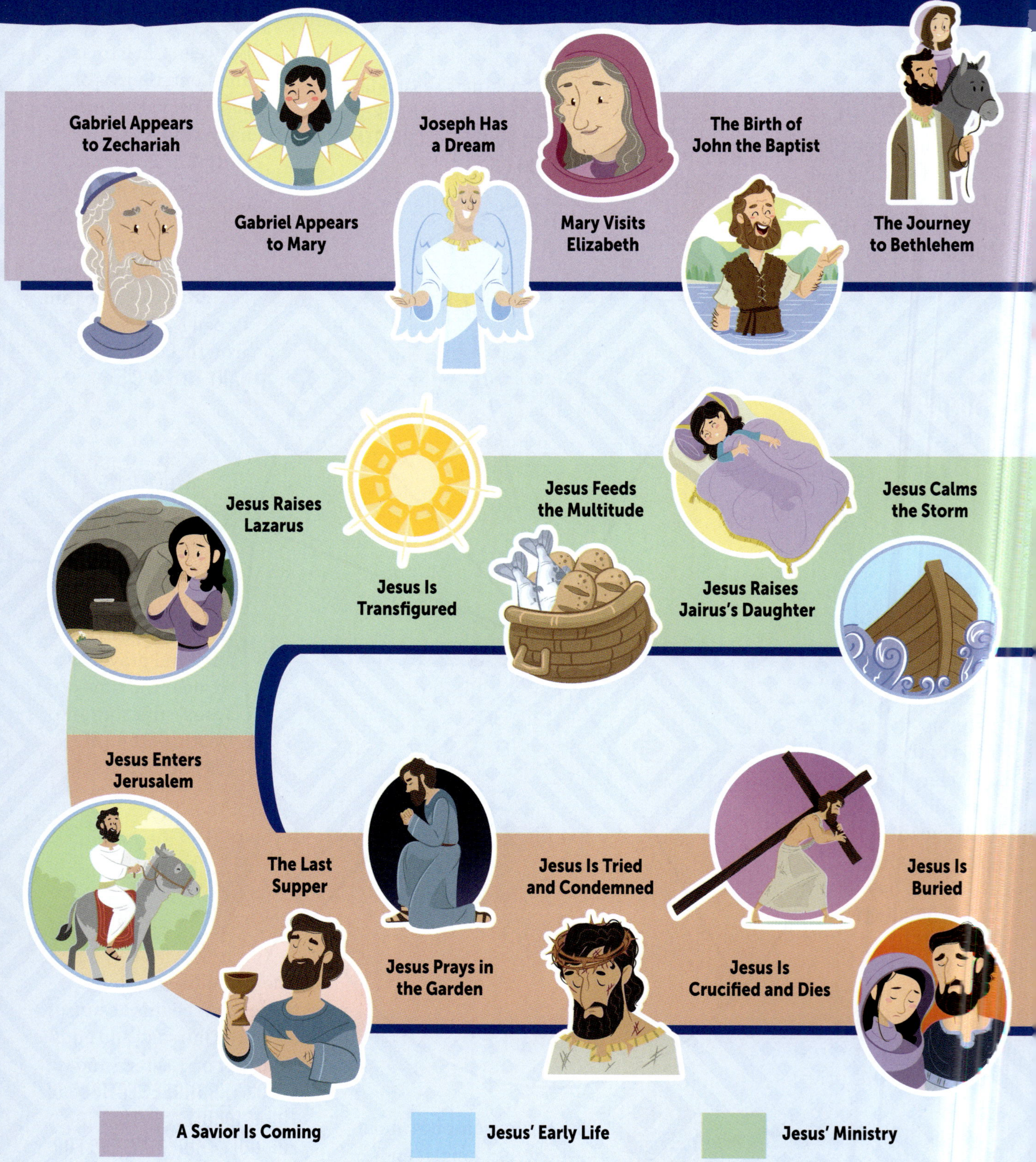

Illustrations by Justin Dial

AUGUST 2026 SUNDAY	MONDAY	TUESDAY
2 **18th SUNDAY IN ORDINARY TIME** Mt 14:13-21 *What is Jesus asking of me when he says, "You give them something to eat"? How can I respond with my students?*	**3**	**4** St. John Vianney
9 **19th SUNDAY IN ORDINARY TIME** Mt 14:22-33 *What might Jesus be asking of you today?*	**10** St. Lawrence, Martyr	**11** St. Clare
16 **20th SUNDAY IN ORDINARY TIME** Mt 15:21-28 *What request do you bring before Jesus in faith?*	**17**	**18**
23 **21st SUNDAY IN ORDINARY TIME** Mt 16:13-20 *Who do you say that Jesus is?*	**24** St. Bartholomew, Apostle	**25** St. Louis; St. Joseph Calasanz
30 **22nd SUNDAY IN ORDINARY TIME** Mt 16:21-27 *How can you help your students name their crosses, take up their crosses, and follow Jesus?*	**31**	

"This Vatican Council declares that the human person has a right to religious freedom." (DH 2)

WEDNESDAY	THURSDAY	FRIDAY	SATURDAY
			1 St. Alphonsus Ligouri
5 The Dedication of the Basilica of St. Mary Major	**6** **THE TRANSFIGURATION OF THE LORD** Mt 17:1-9	**7** St. Sixtus II, Pope, and Companions, Martyrs; St. Cajetan	**8** St. Dominic
12 St. Jane Frances de Chantal	**13** St. Pontian, Pope, and Hippolytus, Martyrs	**14** St. Maximilian Kolbe, Martyr	**15** **THE ASSUMPTION OF THE BLESSED VIRGIN MARY** Lk 1:39-56
19 St. John Eudes	**20** St. Bernard, Doctor of the Church	**21** St. Pius X, Pope	**22** The Queenship of the Blessed Virgin Mary
26	**27** St. Monica	**28** St. Augustine, Doctor of the Church	**29** The Passion of St. John the Baptist

"No one is to be forced to act in a manner contrary to his own beliefs, whether privately or publicly." (DH 2)

Photos: (top) CC Lothar Wolleh (bottom) George Martell/Bayard, Inc.

SEPTEMBER 2026 SUNDAY	MONDAY	TUESDAY
"The right to religious freedom has its foundation in the very dignity of the human person." (DH 2)		**1**
6 **23rd SUNDAY IN ORDINARY TIME** Mt 18:15-20 *How can you make a firm commitment to pray often with your students?*	**7**	**8** The Nativity of the Blessed Virgin Mary Mt 1:1-16, 18-23
13 **24th SUNDAY IN ORDINARY TIME** Mt 18:21-35 *Who do you need to forgive?*	**14** The Exaltation of the Holy Cross Jn 3:13-17	**15** Our Lady of Sorrows
20 **25th SUNDAY IN ORDINARY TIME** Mt 20:1-16a *Do you work out of love for God or out of seeking an expected reward?*	**21** St. Matthew, Apostle	**22**
27 **26th SUNDAY IN ORDINARY TIME** Mt 21:28-32 *In what ways do I see myself in both of the sons in Jesus' parable?*	**28** St. Wenceslaus, Martyr; St. Lawrence Ruiz and Companions, Martyrs	**29** Sts. Michael, Gabriel and Raphael, Archangels

SEPTEMBER 2026

WEDNESDAY	THURSDAY	FRIDAY	SATURDAY
2	3 St. Gregory the Great, Pope and Doctor of the Church	4	5 St. Teresa of Calcutta
9 St. Peter Claver	10	11	12 The Most Holy Name of Mary
16 Sts. Cornelius, Pope, Cyprian, Bishop, Martyrs	17 St. Robert Bellarmine, Doctor of the Church; St. Hildegard of Bingen, Doctor of the Church	18	19 St. Januarius, Martyr
23 St. Pius of Pietrelcina	24	25	26 Sts. Cosmas and Damian, Martyrs
30 St. Jerome, Doctor of the Church			

"The highest norm of human life is the divine law—eternal, objective and universal." (DH 3)

Photos: George Martell/Bayard, Inc.

OCTOBER 2026 SUNDAY	MONDAY	TUESDAY

"Parents have the right to determine, in accordance with their own religious beliefs, the kind of religious education that their children are to receive." (DH 5)

SUNDAY	MONDAY	TUESDAY
4 **27th SUNDAY IN ORDINARY TIME** Mt 21:33-43 *How might I bear fruit for the kingdom of God?*	**5** St. Faustina Kowalska; Bl. Francis Xavier Seelost	**6** St. Bruno; Bl. Marie Rose Durocher
11 **28th SUNDAY IN ORDINARY TIME** Mt 22:1-14 *Am I paying attention to God's invitation in my life?*	**12** St. Carlo Acutis	**13**
18 **29th SUNDAY IN ORDINARY TIME** Mt 22:15-21 *How often do I worry about money or paying debts?*	**19** Sts. John de Brébeuf and Isaac Jogues and Companions, Martyrs	**20** St. Paul of the Cross
25 **30th SUNDAY IN ORDINARY TIME** Mt 22:34-40 *What real-life examples of love of neighbor and reconciliation can I use in classroom or home discussions?*	**26**	**27**

OCTOBER 2026

WEDNESDAY	THURSDAY	FRIDAY	SATURDAY
	1 St. Thérèse of the Child Jesus, Doctor of the Church	2 The Holy Guardian Angels	3
7 Our Lady of the Rosary	8	9 St. John Henry Newman, Doctor of the Church; St. Denis and Companions, Martyrs; St. John Leonardi	10
14 St. Callistus I, Pope and Martyr	15 St. Teresa of Jesus, Doctor of the Church	16 St. Hedwig; St. Margaret Mary Alacoque	17 St. Ignatius of Antioch, Martyr
21	22 St. John Paul II, Pope	23 St. John of Capistrano	24 St. Anthony Mary Claret
28 Sts. Simon and Jude, Apostles	29	30	31

Photos: George Martell/Bayard, Inc.

NOVEMBER 2026 SUNDAY	MONDAY	TUESDAY
1 ALL SAINTS Mt 5:1-12a *How can I be a blessing for my students?*	**2** All Souls' Day	**3** St. Martin de Porres
8 32nd SUNDAY IN ORDINARY TIME Mt 25:1-13 *Have I contemplated my readiness to meet the Lord?*	**9** The Dedication of the Lateran Basilica	**10** St. Leo the Great, Pope and Doctor of the Church
15 33rd SUNDAY IN ORDINARY TIME Mt 25:14-30 *What fears keep me from being charitable?*	**16** St. Margaret of Scotland; St. Gertrude, Virgin	**17** St. Elizabeth of Hungary
22 OUR LORD JESUS CHRIST, KING OF THE UNIVERSE Mt 25:31-46 *How can I help my students recognize different kinds of hunger and thirst?*	**23** St. Clement I, Pope and Martyr; St. Columban, Abbot; Bl. Miguel Agustín Pro, Martyr	**24** St. Andrew Dũng-Lạc and Companions, Martyrs
29 1st SUNDAY OF ADVENT Mk 13:33-37 *Am I complacent about the Second Coming of Jesus Christ?*	**30** St. Andrew, Apostle	

NOVEMBER 2026

WEDNESDAY	THURSDAY	FRIDAY	SATURDAY
4 St. Charles Borromeo	5	6	7
11 St. Martin of Tours	12 St. Josaphat	13 St. Frances Xavier Cabrini	14
18 The Dedication of the Basilicas of Sts. Peter and Paul; St. Rose Philippine Duchesne	19	20	21 The Presentation of the Blessed Virgin Mary
25 St. Catherine of Alexandria	26 Thanksgiving Day, USA	27	28

"Government is to assume the safeguard of the religious freedom of all its citizens, in an effective manner." (DH 6)

Photo: anarch/adobe

ATTENDANCE LOG

NAME OF STUDENT date:	1wk	2wk	3wk	4wk	5wk	6wk	7wk	8wk	9wk	10wk	11wk	12wk	13wk	14wk	15wk
1.															
2.															
3.															
4.															
5.															
6.															
7.															
8.															
9.															
10.															
11.															
12.															
13.															
14.															
15.															
16.															
17.															
18.															
19.															
20.															
21.															
22.															
23.															
24.															
25.															

16wk	17wk	18wk	19wk	20wk	21wk	22wk	23wk	24wk	25wk	26wk	27wk	28wk	29wk	30wk	31wk	32wk	33wk	34wk	35wk	36wk

DECEMBER 2026

"Equality of citizens before the law is never to be violated for religious reasons." (DH 6)

SUNDAY	MONDAY	TUESDAY
		1
6 **2nd SUNDAY OF ADVENT** Mk 1:1-8 *How can I help my students remain focused on the true meaning of the season of Advent?*	7 St. Ambrose, Bishop and Doctor of the Church	8 **THE IMMACULATE CONCEPTION OF THE BLESSED VIRGIN MARY** Lk 1:26-38
13 **3rd SUNDAY OF ADVENT** Jn 1:6-8, 19-28 *Describe the quality of John the Baptist's faith. Why is his message important?*	14 St. John of the Cross, Doctor of the Church	15
20 **4th SUNDAY OF ADVENT** Lk 1:26-38 *How does the coming of Jesus at Christmas inspire hope in you?*	21 St. Peter Canisius, Doctor of the Church	22
27 **THE HOLY FAMILY OF JESUS, MARY, AND JOSEPH** Lk 2:22-40 *Pray for guidance to do the right thing when troubles come my way. Ask the Holy Family to intercede for my most important intention today.*	28 The Holy Innocents, Martyrs	29 St. Thomas Becket, Bishop and Martyr

DECEMBER 2026

WEDNESDAY	THURSDAY	FRIDAY	SATURDAY
2	3 St. Francis Xavier	4 St. John Damascene, Doctor of the Church	5
9 St. Juan Diego Cuauhtlatoatzin	10 Our Lady of Loreto	11 St. Damasus I, Pope	12 Our Lady of Guadalupe
16	17	18	19
23 St. John of Kanty	24	25 **THE NATIVITY OF THE LORD** Vigil: Mt 1:1-25 Night: Lk 2:1-14 Dawn: Lk 2:15-20 Day: Jn 1:1-18 *Remember that Christmas = Christ's Mass. Rejoice that Jesus comes at Christmas and at every Mass to love us forever.*	26 St. Stephen, the First Martyr
30	31 St. Sylvester I, Pope		

Photo: peopleimages.com/Adobe

JANUARY 2027

"A wrong is done when government imposes upon its people the profession or repudiation of any religion." (DH 6)

SUNDAY	MONDAY	TUESDAY
3 THE EPIPHANY OF THE LORD Mt 2:1-12 *How can I help my students explore their personal gifts so that they, too, might "open their treasures" and offer them to the Christ Child?*	**4** St. Elizabeth Ann Seton	**5** St. John Neumann
10 THE BAPTISM OF THE LORD Mk 1:7-11 *How can I help my students understand their identity as beloved children of God, like Jesus at his baptism?*	**11**	**12**
17 2ND SUNDAY IN ORDINARY TIME Jn 1:35-42 **Sunday of the Word of God** *Who is the Lamb of God, and how can we find him today?*	**18**	**19**
24 3RD SUNDAY IN ORDINARY TIME Mk 1:14-20 *What have you left behind in order to follow Jesus?*	**25** The Conversion of Saint Paul the Apostle	**26** Sts. Timothy and Titus
31 4th SUNDAY IN ORDINARY TIME Mk 1:21-28 *Pray for the courage and confidence to teach as Jesus taught.*		

JANUARY 2027

WEDNESDAY	THURSDAY	FRIDAY	SATURDAY
		1 SOLEMNITY OF MARY, THE HOLY MOTHER OF GOD Lk 2:16-21	**2** Sts. Basil and Gregory, Doctors of the Church
6 St. André Bessette	**7** St. Raymond of Penyafort	**8**	**9**
13 St. Hilary, Doctor of the Church	**14**	**15**	**16**
20 St. Fabian, Pope; St. Sebastian, Martyr	**21** St. Agnes	**22** Day of Prayer for the Legal Protection of Unborn Children	**23** St. Vincent, Martyr; St. Marianne Cope
27 St. Angela Merici	**28** St. Thomas Aquinas, Doctor of the Church	**29**	**30**

"The act of faith is of its very nature a free act." (DH 10)

Photos: (top) George Martell/Bayard, Inc. (bottom) Lisa Julia Photography/Bayard, Inc.

FEBRUARY 2027 SUNDAY	MONDAY	TUESDAY
	1	2 The Presentation of the Lord
7 **5th SUNDAY IN ORDINARY TIME** Mk 1:29-39 *What experience from my own life can I share with my students about the strength found in Jesus' healing touch?*	8 St. Jerome Emiliani; St. Josephine Bakhita	9
14 **1st SUNDAY OF LENT** Mk 1:12-15 *How is Lent akin to Jesus' desert time?*	15	16
21 **2nd SUNDAY OF LENT** Mk 9:2-10 *How do the Father's words about Jesus apply to me?*	22 The Chair of Saint Peter the Apostle	23 St. Polycarp, Martyr
28 **3rdSUNDAY OF LENT** Jn 2:13-25 *How might I explain to my students my zeal for the Catholic faith and the Church?*		

WEDNESDAY	THURSDAY	FRIDAY	SATURDAY
3 St. Blaise, Martyr; St. Ansgar	4	5 St. Agatha, Martyr	6 St. Paul Miki and Companions, Martyrs
10 Ash Wednesday	11 Our Lady of Lourdes	12	13
17 The Seven Holy Founders of the Servite Order	18	19	20
24	25	26	27 St. Gregory of Narek, Doctor of the Church

"No one therefore is to be forced to embrace the Christian faith against his own will." (DH 10)

Photos: George Martell/Bayard, Inc.

MARCH 2027 SUNDAY	MONDAY	TUESDAY
	1	2
7 **4th SUNDAY OF LENT** Jn 3:14-21 *What is the deepest darkness to which I bring the light of Jesus?*	8 St. John of God	9 St. Frances of Rome
14 **5th SUNDAY OF LENT** Jn 12:20-33 *Is there something more that the Lord is calling me to this Lent?*	15	16
21 **PALM SUNDAY OF THE PASSION OF THE LORD** Mk 14:1—15:47 *How are we sleeping in our faith?*	22	23
28 **EASTER SUNDAY OF THE RESURRECTION OF THE LORD** Jn 20:1-9 *How does the empty tomb energize my faith?*	29 Monday within the Octave of Easter	30 Tuesday within the Octave of Easter

WEDNESDAY	THURSDAY	FRIDAY	SATURDAY
3 St. Katharine Drexel	4 St. Casimir	5	6
10	11	12	13
17 St. Patrick	18 St. Cyril of Jerusalem, Doctor of the Church	19 **ST. JOSEPH, SPOUSE OF THE BLESSED VIRGIN MARY**	20
24	25 Holy Thursday	26 Good Friday	27 Holy Saturday
31 Wednesday within the Octave of Easter			

MARCH 2027

"Render to Caesar the things that are Caesar's and to God the things that are God's." (DH 11, quoting Matt. 22:21)

Photos: George Martell/Bayard, Inc.

APRIL 2027 SUNDAY	MONDAY	TUESDAY
4 **2nd SUNDAY OF EASTER or Sunday of Divine Mercy** Jn 20:19-31 *In what specific ways am I helping my students to celebrate the entire Easter Season?*	**5** **THE ANNUNCIATION OF THE LORD**	**6**
11 **3rd SUNDAY OF EASTER** Lk 24:35-48 *Today I meditate on the holy wounds of Jesus and the unconditional love they represent.*	**12**	**13** St. Martin I, Pope and Martyr
18 **4th SUNDAY OF EASTER** Jn 10:11-18 *How does the image of Jesus as the Good Shepherd inspire my ministry as a catechist?*	**19**	**20**
25 **5th SUNDAY OF EASTER** Jn 15:1-8 *What is Jesus saying to me in my ministry as a catechist?*	**26**	**27**

"The common good consists chiefly in the safeguarding of the rights and duties of the human person." (DH 6)

APRIL 2027

WEDNESDAY	THURSDAY	FRIDAY	SATURDAY
	1 Thursday within the Octave of Easter	2 Friday within the Octave of Easter	3 Saturday within the Octave of Easter
7 St. John Baptist de la Salle	8	9	10
14	15	16	17
21 St. Anselm, Doctor of the Church	22	23 St George, Martyr; St. Adalbert, Martyr	24 St. Fidelis of Sigmaringen, Martyr
28 St. Peter Chanel; St. Louis Grignion de Montfort	29 St. Catherine of Siena, Doctor of the Church	30 St. Pius V, Pope	

Photo: rawpixel.com/Adobe

MAY 2027 SUNDAY	MONDAY	TUESDAY

"Christ gave His Apostles the command to preach the Gospel to every creature." (DH 11)

SUNDAY	MONDAY	TUESDAY
2 **6th SUNDAY OF EASTER** Jn 15:9-17 *Who do I find most difficult to love?*	**3** Sts. Philip and James, Apostles	**4**
9 **THE ASCENSION OF THE LORD** Mk 16:15-20 *How might I pray for each of my students by name today?*	**10** St. John De Avila, Doctor of the Church; St. Damien de Veuster	**11**
16 **PENTECOST SUNDAY** Jn 20:19-23 *I pray to be filled by the Holy Spirit and to know the joy of the Lord.*	**17** The Blessed Virgin Mary, Mother of the Church	**18** St. John I, Pope and Martyr
23 **THE MOST HOLY TRINITY** Mt 28:16-20 *How can I help my students understand Jesus' promise to be with us always?*	**24**	**25** St. Bede the Venerable, Doctor of the Church; St. Gregory VII, Pope; St. Mary Magdalene de' Paz
30 **THE MOST HOLY BODY AND BLOOD OF CHRIST** Mk 14:12-16, 22-26 *Examine your schedule this week and commit to more prayer in front of the Blessed Sacrament or more frequent daily Mass.*	**31** The Visitation of the Blessed Virgin Mary	

WEDNESDAY	THURSDAY	FRIDAY	SATURDAY
			1 St. Joseph the Worker
5	6 **THE ASCENSION OF THE LORD** *This Holy Day of Obligation applies only to the ecclesial provinces of Boston, Hartford, New York, Omaha, and Philadelphia. Other dioceses will celebrate the Ascension on Sunday, May 9.	7	8
12 Sts. Nereus and Achilleus; St. Pancras	13 Our Lady of Fatima	14 St. Matthias, Apostle	15 St. Isidore
19	20 St. Bernardine of Siena	21 St. Christopher Magallanes and Companions, Martyrs	22 St. Rita of Cascia
26 St. Philip Neri	27 St. Augustine of Canterbury	28	29 St. Paul VI, Pope

"The freedom of the Church is the fundamental principle in what concerns the relations between the Church and governments." (DH 13)

Photos: (Top) Renáta Sedmáková/Adobe (bottom) fotomaster/Adobe

JUNE 2027

SUNDAY	MONDAY	TUESDAY
		1 St. Justin, Martyr
6 **10th SUNDAY IN ORDINARY TIME** Mk 3:20-35 *What does today's Gospel teach us about the nature of family and the importance of obeying God's will?*	**7**	**8**
13 **11th SUNDAY IN ORDINARY TIME** Mk 4:26-34 *Which parable might I reflect on through the summer to enrich my ministry as a catechist next year?*	**14**	**15**
20 **12th SUNDAY IN ORDINARY TIME** Mk 4:35-41 *What storms am I facing — and how can I better turn to Jesus as I face them?*	**21** St. Aloysius Gonzaga	**22** St. Paulinus of Nola; Sts. John Fisher and Thomas More, Martyrs
27 **13th SUNDAY IN ORDINARY TIME** Mk 5:21-43 *What impossible situations ought I bring to Jesus?*	**28** St. Irenaeus, Bishop, Martyr, and Doctor of the Church	**29** **STS. PETER AND PAUL, APOSTLES**

WEDNESDAY	THURSDAY	FRIDAY	SATURDAY
2 Sts. Marcellinus and Peter	3 St. Charles Lwanga and Companions, Martyrs	4 **THE MOST SACRED HEART OF JESUS**	5 The Immaculate Heart of the Blessed Virgin Mary; St. Boniface, Martyr
9 St. Ephrem, Doctor of the Church	10	11 St. Barnabas, Apostle	12
16	17	18	19 St. Romuald
23	24 **THE NATIVITY OF SAINT JOHN THE BAPTIST**	25	26
30 The First Martyrs of the Holy Roman Church			

"The Church herself is the first to recognize and defend the freedom of the human person." (DH 13)

Photo: Vatican Pool/Gettyimages

Creating a Lesson Plan

Catechists ought to be conscientious and intentional regarding lesson planning. Lesson plans are important tools and critical for our success. Lesson planning organizes our efforts, respects time constraints, and maximizes students' learning and growth in faith. Yet the heart of our lessons ought to be grounded in our own prayerful preparation and how we will share Christ with our students. Therefore, the lesson plan contains both spiritual goals as well as learning goals. (See template on the opposite page. Photocopy it or download it at *Catechist.com/LessonPlan.*)

OVERVIEW OF OBJECTIVES: *How will you witness to the faith in this lesson?*

SPIRITUAL GOALS: What makes catechesis different from other forms of learning is that the object of catechesis is communion with Jesus Christ. It promotes an encounter with Christ through our beliefs, the sacraments, the moral life, and the life of prayer. "At the heart of catechesis we find, in essence, a Person, the Person of Jesus of Nazareth," (Pope Saint John Paul II, *Catechesi Tradendae,* 5).

Try preparing with these questions:

- How might I foster an encounter with Christ for my students?
- How will I/we pray?
- What is the biblical basis for this lesson?
- Is there a connection to the Liturgical Year or Sunday Mass?

LEARNING GOALS: This is what we want students to know, demonstrate, and/or better understand at the end of a lesson. Objectives usually are measurable in some way, and so the learning objective must be clear and specific—and kept in mind while building the remainder of the lesson plan.

RELEVANCE: This makes the faith-and-life connection, making the lesson meaningful. What students know, demonstrate, and/or better understand at the end of a lesson must relate to their daily lives and the way they live and celebrate their Catholic faith.

Keys to relevance:

1: Understand the developmental stage of the students in the class or group.

2: Uncover the *why* of the lesson that answers, "So what?"

3: Assess whether, ultimately, this lesson solves a problem that the students might have or offers a gift for students' lives.

PRESENTATION: *How will you implement the lesson's objectives?*

INTRODUCTION: This might be a prayer, drama, piece of music, story, or activity that captures students' attention in the first minutes of class.

CONNECTION: This is the bridge that connects the introduction with the rest of the lesson. A great introduction and great content are weakened if students don't understand how they are connected. The connection often is a brief, one-sentence statement that helps students make associations between the two.

CONTENT: This is the body of the lesson in which new information is presented or previously presented material is reviewed—or both. Good content is strengthened with creative examples, open-ended questions, Scripture references, and details that engage students.

ACTIVITY: Depending on students' ages, this may be a discussion, game, worksheet, skit, arts-and-crafts project, reflection, or any experience that reviews and reinforces the content.

CLOSURE: *How will you wrap up the lesson in a memorable way?*

FEEDBACK: This is any exercise that helps you determine how well learners have grasped the new information presented.

SENDING FORTH: This prayer, song, or celebrative moment sends students forth with joy, ready to live what they learned and experienced in class. Finally, suggest how students can put their faith into practice this week in prayer or action. Make the faith-life connection real!

REFERENCE TEXTS AND MATERIALS NEEDED: *Be prepared!*

Be sure to write down all your reference notes and supply needs for each aspect of the lesson plan. Arrive to class early to organize your notes and reference texts and to make sure all materials needed to present the lesson are available and/or operational. Double-check that any students' needed supplies are on hand.

LESSON PLAN

DATE: __________

OVERVIEW OF OBJECTIVES: *How will I witness to the faith in this lesson?*

Spiritual goals: *How might I foster an encounter with Christ for my students?* ______________________________

____

How will I/we pray? ____

What is the biblical basis for this lesson? ____

Is there a connection to the Liturgical Year or Sunday Mass? __________________________

Learning goals: *What do I wish my students to learn? List 1-2 important ideas for children, 3 for older youth and adults.*

____

____

____

Relevance of the content: *Why is this important?* _______________________________

PRESENTATION: *Implementing the Objectives*

Introduction (time: ______ **):**

____

____

Connection: _________________________________

Content (time: ______ **):** _____________________

____

____

____

____

____

____

____

Activity (time: ______ **):** ____________________

____

CLOSURE: *Ending the lesson well*

Feedback (time: ______ **):** ___________________

____

Sending forth (time: ______ **):** _______________

Suggestion for putting faith into practice: ____________

____

Reference texts/Materials needed:
(Bible? Textbook? Prayers? Catechism? Supplies? A/V? Technology? Announcements?)

____

____

____

____

____

____

____

____

____

____

____

____

____

____

____

____

____

____

Prayers for Lesson Prep

THE JESUS PRAYER

by St. John Henry Newman

Dear Jesus,
Help me to spread your fragrance everywhere I go. Flood my soul with your spirit and life. Penetrate and possess my whole being so utterly, that my life may only be a radiance of yours.

Shine through me, and be so in me that every soul I come in contact with may feel your presence in my soul. Let them look up and see no longer me but only Jesus!

Stay with me and then I shall begin to shine as you shine, so to shine as to be a light to others; the light, O Jesus, will be all from you; none of it will be mine; it will be you shining on others through me. Amen.

PRAYER TO THE HOLY SPIRIT

Come, Holy Spirit, fill the hearts of your faithful.
And kindle in them the fire of your love.
Send forth your Spirit and they shall be created.
And you shall renew the face of the earth.
Let us pray:
O God, by the light of the Holy Spirit
you have taught the hearts of your faithful.
In the same Spirit, help us to know what is truly right and always to rejoice in your consolation.
We ask this through Christ, Our Lord. Amen.

Books of the Bible

OLD TESTAMENT

PENTATEUCH

Genesis (Gn)
Exodus (Ex)
Leviticus (Lv)
Numbers (Nm)
Deuteronomy (Dt)

HISTORICAL BOOKS

Joshua (Jos)
Judges (Jgs)
Ruth (Ru)
1 Samuel (1 Sm)
2 Samuel (2 Sm)
1 Kings (1 Kgs)
2 Kings (2 Kgs)
1 Chronicles (1 Chr)
2 Chronicles (2 Chr)
Ezra (Ezr)
Nehemiah (Neh)
Tobit (Tb)
Judith (Jdt)
Esther (Est)
1 Maccabees (1 Mc)
2 Maccabees (2 Mc)

WISDOM BOOKS

Job (Jb)
Psalms (Ps or Pss)
Proverbs (Prv)
Ecclesiastes (Eccl)
Song of Songs (Song or Sg)
Wisdom (Wis)
Sirach/ Ecclesiasticus (Sir)

PROPHETIC BOOKS

Isaiah (Is)
Jeremiah (Jer)
Lamentations (Lam)
Baruch (Bar)
Ezekiel (Ez)
Daniel (Dn)
Hosea (Hos)
Joel (Jl)
Amos (Am)
Obadiah (Ob)
Jonah (Jon)
Micah (Mi)
Nahum (Na)
Habakkuk (Hb)
Zephaniah (Zep)
Haggai (Hg)
Zechariah (Zec)
Malachi (Mal)

NEW TESTAMENT

GOSPELS

Matthew (Mt)
Mark (Mk)
Luke (Lk)
John (Jn)

HISTORY

Acts of the Apostles (Acts)

NEW TESTAMENT LETTERS

Romans (Rom)
1 Corinthians (1 Cor)
2 Corinthians (2 Cor)
Galatians (Gal)
Ephesians (Eph)
Philippians (Phil)
Colossians (Col)
1 Thessalonians (1 Thes)
2 Thessalonians (2 Thes)
1 Timothy (1 Tm)
2 Timothy (2 Tm)
Titus (Ti)
Philemon (Phlm)
Hebrews (Heb)

CATHOLIC LETTERS

James (Jas)
1 Peter (1 Pt)
2 Peter (2 Pt)
1 John (1 Jn)
2 John (2 Jn)
3 John (3 Jn)
Jude (Jude)

REVELATION

Revelation (Rv)

PHOTO: ANELINA/SHUTTERSTOCK